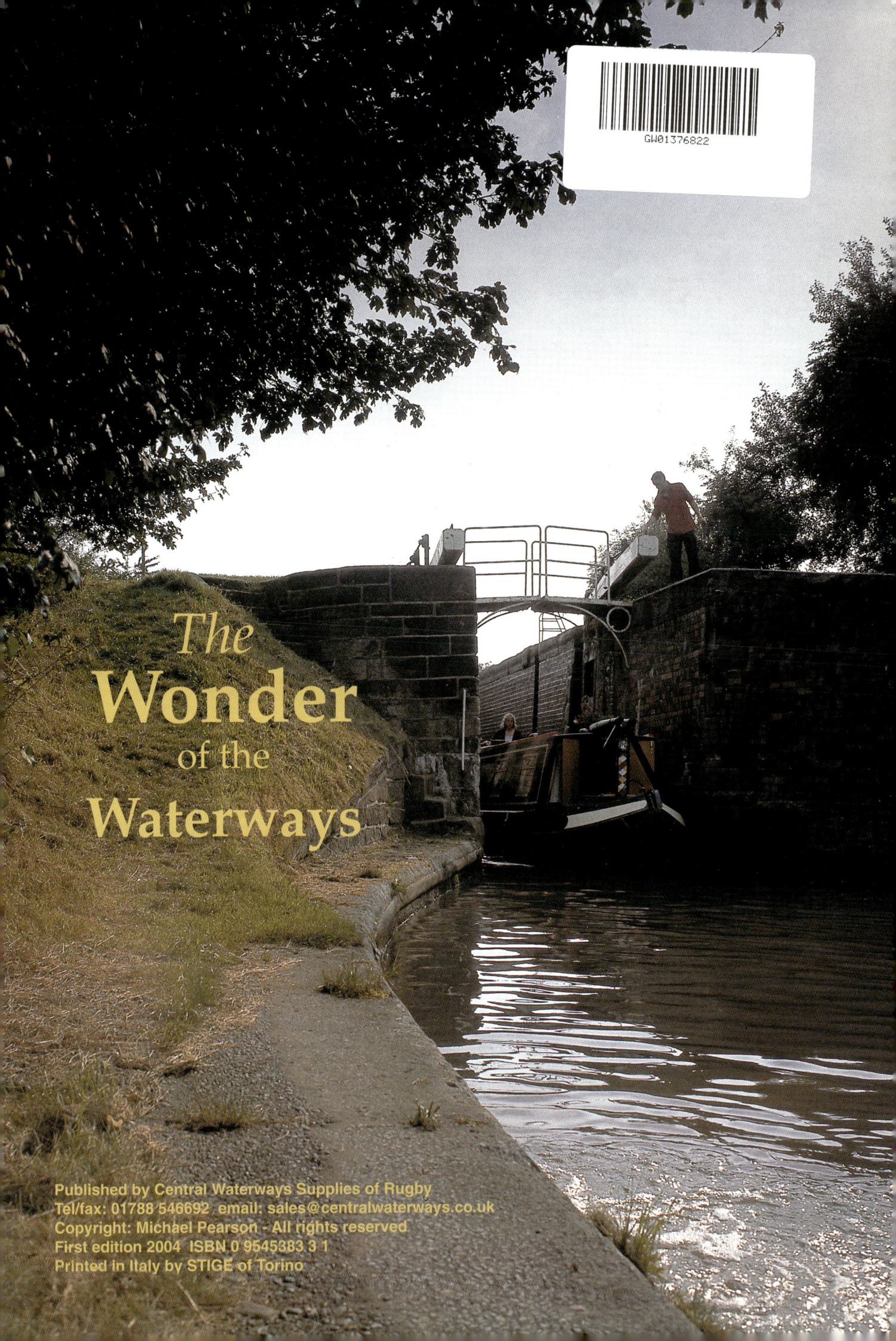

The Wonder of the Waterways

Published by Central Waterways Supplies of Rugby
Tel/fax: 01788 546692 email: sales@centralwaterways.co.uk
Copyright: Michael Pearson - All rights reserved
First edition 2004 ISBN 0 9545383 3 1
Printed in Italy by STIGE of Torino

The Wonder of the Waterways

The wonder of the waterways is that they survived at all. Many of Britain's canals and river navigations were acquired by railway interests in the 19th century to stifle competition. A long slow decline followed, typically with abandonment at the end of it. Two world wars artificially prolonged commercial trade on certain routes - notably the Grand Union Canal between London and Birmingham - but if it hadn't been for the formation of the Inland Waterways Association in 1946, inspired by L. T. C. Rolt's seminal book *Narrow Boat* , it is hard to escape the frightening truth that the bulk of the inland waterway system in this country would have vanished from the map before the leisure age dawned.

So it is perhaps nothing short of miraculous that, at the beginning of the 21st Century, three thousand linear miles of canals and river navigations provide a recreational outlet unimagined by their 18th Century promoters and engineers, for whom the carriage of cargoes was paramount. Canal boating as a holiday activity didn't really get underway until the 1960s, though there had been pioneering attempts to encourage leisure use of the canals along the lines of the River Thames and Norfolk Broads in the 1930s. Walking and cycling beside canals, together with the enjoyment of their industrial archaeology are even more recent phenomenons, and now millions of people per annum derive enjoyment from visiting our inland waterways.

Fresh momentum is attracting itself to the canal network at the beginning of the 21st century in the form of regeneration. Several notable routes which no one imagined would ever become navigable again have been fully restored in recent years and more look set to follow. Projects, like the restoration of the Forth & Clyde and Union canals in Scotland and the Huddersfield and Rochdale canals in England, are not simply undertaken to expand the mileage of the system for the benefit of boaters, but more importantly to help bring life and commerce back to areas which have suffered post-industrially more than most. And however you choose to define the phenomenon, a working waterway on one's doorstep does have the happy knack of bringing economic confidence and a life-enhancing atmosphere in its wake.

This book attempts to introduce a taste of the canal network to newcomers, and to remind old hands of its inherent pleasures. Within its slim covers it barely skims the surface of its subject matter for which a growing number of scholarly books are becoming available to those who wish to learn more. Modestly we might point you in the direction of the *Pearson's Canal Companion* series of guide books if you are beginning to think you'd enjoy becoming more closely acquainted with the canal system. For over twenty years they've been guiding boaters, walkers, cyclists and motorists alike around the system, examining its heritage, illuminating its context in the landscape, and offering practical advice from the location of the nearest bus stop to the likely quality of the bitter at the Red Bull. Happy canaling!

Beau Bridges

THE humble humpbacked bridge is perhaps the most quintessential image of the British canal network. Why else would British Waterways, the guardians of the system, incorporate it in their logo? Such bridges were built to carry public rights of way across the new canal, or provided for the 'accommodation' of farmers and landowners, so that their chattels and cattle would not be inconvenienced by the linear moat that had suddenly been cut across their land. Where possible, cost-saving local materials were used, and this together with the passage of time has rendered these throw-backs to the 18th century almost organic in their relationship with the ground they stand on.

Visit almost any canal and you won't have to walk far to see a humpbacked bridge like that seen *(above)* on the Leicester Section of the Grand Union Canal between **Glen Parva** and Aylestone. Through its beguiling arch, or bridge-hole, you can just discern the beams of Blue Banks Lock, the penultimate lock before the canal is joined by the River Soar. Sadly this particular bridge - No.102 in a sequence which commences at Norton Junction near Daventry - seems to have lost its number plate. Bridgeplates, whether they carry simply a number, or a name, are an attractive feature that transcend the mere definition of your whereabouts. **Saint Thomas Bridge**, No.101, on the Staffordshire & Worcestershire Canal near Stafford *(right)* is a case in point. In this instance the numbering begins at Stourport on the River Severn and culminates in No.109, the lovely junction bridge at Great Haywood featured elsewhere in this book.

An alternative method of bridging canals was the construction of a moveable bridge, one which might be made either to lift or to swing: the Llangollen and Oxford canals are best known for the former, the Leeds & Liverpool and the Gloucester & Sharpness for the latter. That so many remain in use is a testament to the strength and endurance of their construction; in recent years

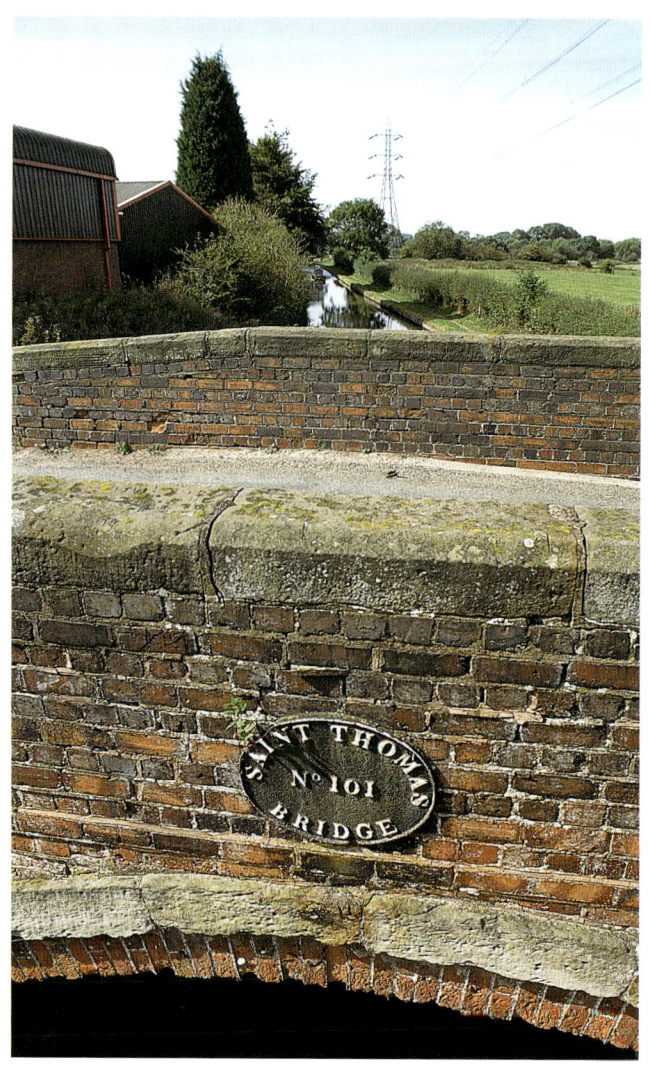

Please lower the bridge after passing through as this is a public footpath. Thank you.

many have been upgraded and made to operate electrically where road traffic is heavy. Others have been rebuilt from timber to steel, but here *(above)* on the outskirts of **Wrenbury** in Cheshire is a picture of the last remaining timber lift-bridge still in use on the main line of the Llangollen Canal, whilst *(left)* less than a mile from the centre of Oxford is one of the stylishly much different yet functionally similar Oxford Canal lift-bridges.

Swing-bridges also come in numerous shapes and sizes: the one photographed *(below)* on the Leeds & Liverpool Canal north of **Rodley** looks as though it's seldom used, but that doesn't detract from its simple dignity. A contrast in fortunes is evident at another

Leeds & Liverpool location, **Skipton** where Bridge No.177 *(left above)* has been electrified, boaters who use it needing to access a control panel by means of a special key provided by British Waterways. It can be an un-nerving business for the rooky boater, and the occasional malfunction can lead to substantial traffic jams of impatient motorists!

A similar situation occurs at **Fools Nook** *(right above)* on the Macclesfield Canal in Cheshire where a milk tanker is shown waiting patiently for a boat to pass. But swing-bridges do bring an added sense of adventure to the canals, and one looks forward to encountering them.

Not only was it necessary for roadways and access tracks between fields to cross the canal, but also the need frequently arose for the towpath to cross water, for example where a feeder came in to the main channel, or an arm from a loading basin.

At **Aynho** - in the bottom left hand corner of Northamptonshire - the River Cherwell briefly crosses the Oxford Canal resulting in an attractive sequence of arches *(below)* carrying the towpath across the river. Just below this point you come across the unusually diamond-shaped Aynho Weir Lock.

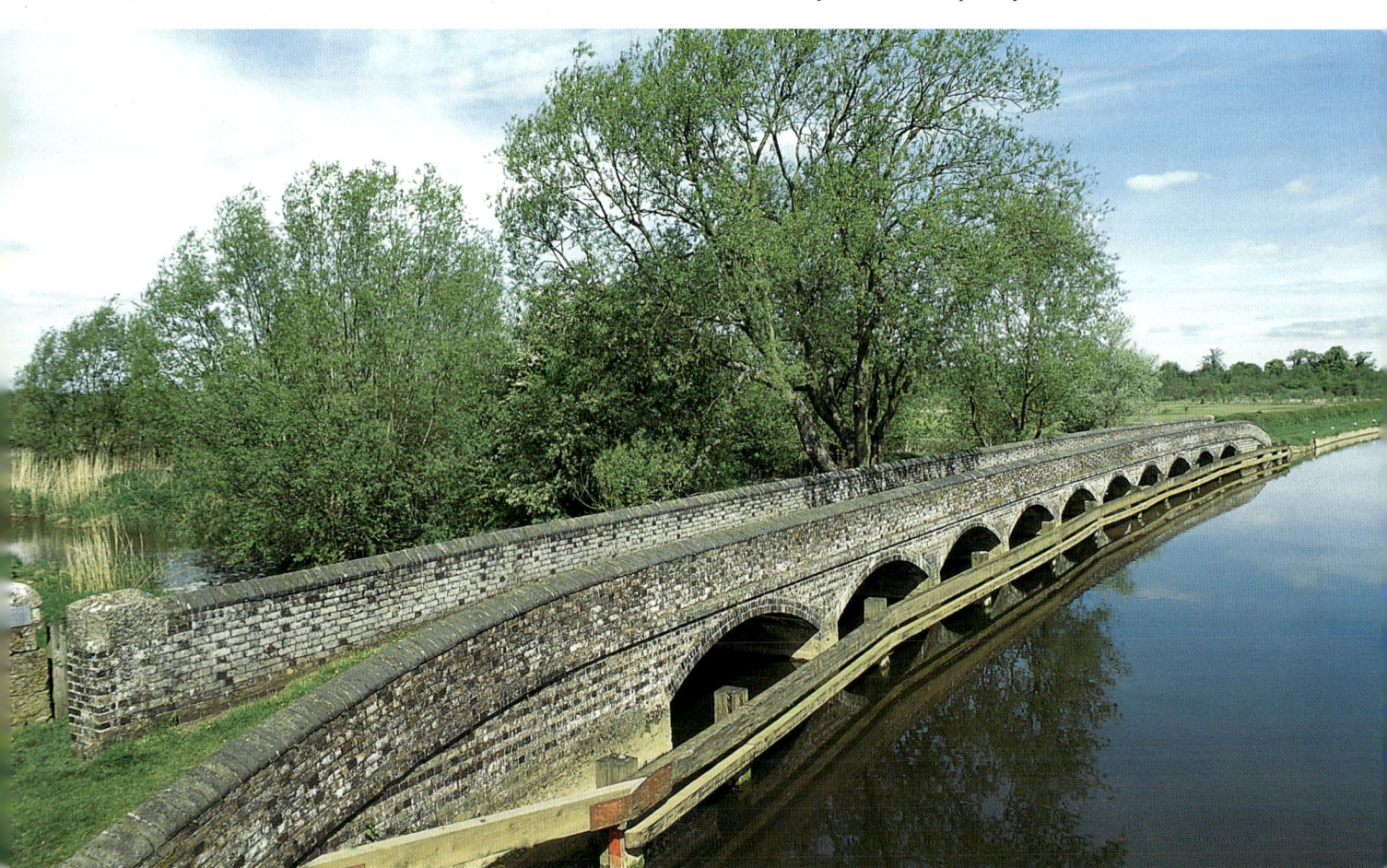

On the Staffordshire & Worcestershire Canal at **Cookley**, an arm of the canal used to provide access to an iron works, one of several located along this now deceptively picturesque waterway. Pictured *(above)* you can see that the works and the main channel of the canal are both very much still in business, but the little iron bridge now crosses a reed-filled arm, no longer navigable by boats. An interesting feature of the Oxford Canal is the use of elegant cast iron bridges to span the original, much-winding route, now mostly reduced to silted arms, such as seen *(below)* near **Brinklow** in Warwickshire. When the old route was effectively by-passed, the arm served a village wharf. The Fellows Morton & Clayton steamer *Earl* was ignominiously abandoned to a marshy grave on the Brinklow Arm in 1931.

At **Braunston**, the same type of bridge *(above)* is used to carry the towpath over the Oxford Canal's Junction with the Grand Union Canal.

Wherever you go on the canals you will encounter an almost infinite variety of engineering, brought about by the calculated response of craftsmen and engineers. Here *(above)* near **Devizes** on the Kennet & Avon Canal is a simple wooden footbridge, yet how appealing it is! Often the design is more specific as *(below)* on the **Stratford-on-Avon Canal** where a cantilevered style developed to facilitate the use of tow lines between the two separate spans of the bridge.

Not all canal bridge designs were engineering-led. Occasionally influential landowners needed to be mollified if the canal was to be dug across their land. Usually ostentation was the by-word as *(above)* on the Trent & Mersey Canal between Stone and Weston-on-Trent. This is Bridge No.82, made especially decorative in brick and stone for the benefit of the nearby estate of **Sandon**.

Of similar motive in its origin is Bridge 65 *(below)* on the Grand Union Canal at **Cosgrove**, a delightfully Gothic construction which, temporarily at any rate, lends the canal the affected dignity of an ornamental lake by Capability Brown. Just south of here a curious little tunnel was provided beneath the canal to permit access from the towpath to a pub called The Barley Mow on the opposite bank of the canal.

A world away in atmosphere from the peaceful Northamptonshire countryside of Cosgrove, Castlefield in **Manchester** *(right)* illustrates the kind of bridge structures which the Railway Age delivered in its wake. The arms which radiate from the Bridgewater Canal are spanned by generations of such bridges, built variously from brick and iron and steel. Though randomly achieved, the effect is exhilarating, and this is definitely an easily accessible location which calls out for exploration.

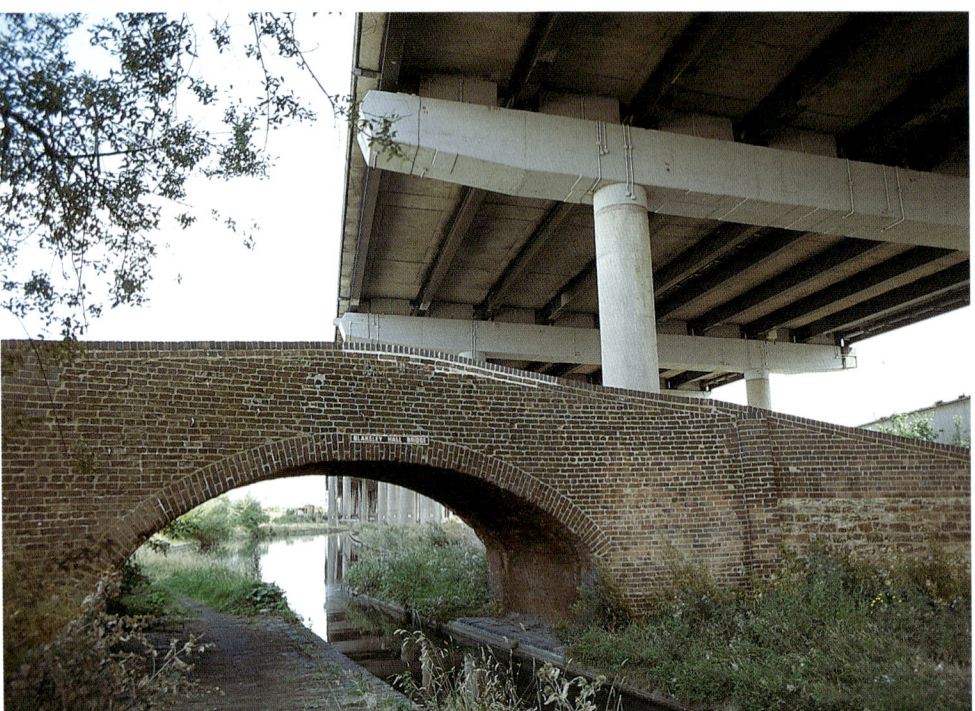

Not quite so easily reached, are sundry corners of the Black Country in the West Midlands where, even if you appear to be in the middle of a conurbation, many canal locations exude a peculiarly remote feel. Two ages of bridge construction confront each other at **Oldbury** *(left)* on the Birmingham Canal Navigations. This is the original Brindley built main line between Birmingham and Wolverhampton still displaying defiantly a humpback bridge despite being dwarfed by the M5 motorway above it. Nearby the main Birmingham-Wolverhampton railway also crosses the canal and you can compare each transport mode's impact on the landscape, drawing your own conclusions as to the most environmentally harmonious method of travel.

How many faithful followers of 'The Reds' spare a glance for the **Bridgewater Canal** *(right)* as they make their way across its oily waters to watch a home game at Old Trafford? Even more significantly, how many of the older fans remember barges using these waters as comparatively recently as 1974, when Kellogg's still utilised water transport to tranship American-grown wheat from Manchester Docks to their factory on the Trafford Park Estate? At least it looks as though someone has made an attempt to lend the bridge some aesthetic value.

The Kennet & Avon Canal, which runs between Bath and Reading, features a wide variety of bridges; ancient and modern alike. The **Bath** flight of locks alone - easily walked beside a short distance from Bath Spa railway station - includes a number of charmingly elegant structures, built so as to meld in with the city's Georgian architecture. This bridge *(left)* can be found at the tail of Lock No.10, delightfully known as Wash House Lock. Nearby, a mere stroll beyond the top lock, the canal romantically skirts the periphery of Sydney Gardens, one of Bath's 18th century 'resorts of pleasure'.

Canal travellers and explorers often concentrate their attention on the design of bridges viewed from the waterside. Yet, inherently, their typically curving parapets are equally pleasing aesthetically seen side on from the aspect of the roadway as here *(right)* at **Alton Barnes** where Bridge No. 124 frames the view of one of Wiltshire's famous chalk horses.

A few hundred yards west of the bridge stands Honey Street Wharf and a very convivial pub called The Barge, an important stopping off point in the canal's working heyday and every bit as popular with canal travellers today as well.

And, finally, just in case you fall into the trap of thinking that the majority of canal bridges are moss and lichen covered humpback affairs, here's *(left)* a modern example of their ilk, a very recent addition to the canal scene in **Reading** where the Oracle Shopping Centre development has thrown up a number of new crossings. It is good to see canals and river navigations being incorporated into new retail developments, but care needs to be exercised to ensure that the relationship is on an equal footing, and that the waterway and its passing boat traffic is not simply viewed as a picturesque addendum to the real business of shopping.

Up & Under

AQUEDUCTS and tunnels are the most incredible features of canal engineering simply because they are the most unexpected. Everybody knows that trains race across high viaducts and plunge into long tunnels, but for newcomers to the canal system, such structures, when first encountered, are an astonishing surprise.

The Welsh end of the Llangollen Canal is as good a place as any to savour the drama and impact of aqueducts and tunnels. **Whitehouses Tunnel** *(above)* is only 191 yards long and has a towpath running through it and so can be sampled on foot, perhaps as part of a thrilling four mile walk between Chirk and Froncysyllte, settlements linked by a regular bus service. From Froncysyllte it's just a short additional distance to one of the most outstanding canal structures in the world, **Pontcysyllte Aqueduct** *(below)* which you can also walk across, always assuming you have a good head for heights, for at its tallest point, Thomas Telford's masterpiece, completed in 1805, stands 127 feet above the River Dee.

Barely less exceptional is the nearby **Chirk Aqueduct** *(opposite upper)* which carries the Llangollen Canal across the valley of the River Ceiriog and the border between England and Wales. It is accompanied on its great leap across the valley by an even taller railway viaduct, a visually exciting juxtaposition which finds itself reprised at **Marple** *(right)* on the outskirts of Stockport where the Peak Forest Canal is carried dramatically over the River Goyt.

The Trent & Mersey Canal is a good one to go boating on if you want to experience a subterranean journey afloat. **Saltersford** *(below)* is one of three tunnels at the northern end of this canal which were amongst the very first dug by Brindley. In those early days of canal construction, engineers lacked confidence to build a towpath through the bore so the boat horses had to follow a path across the top of the hill, the same being true of pedestrians today.

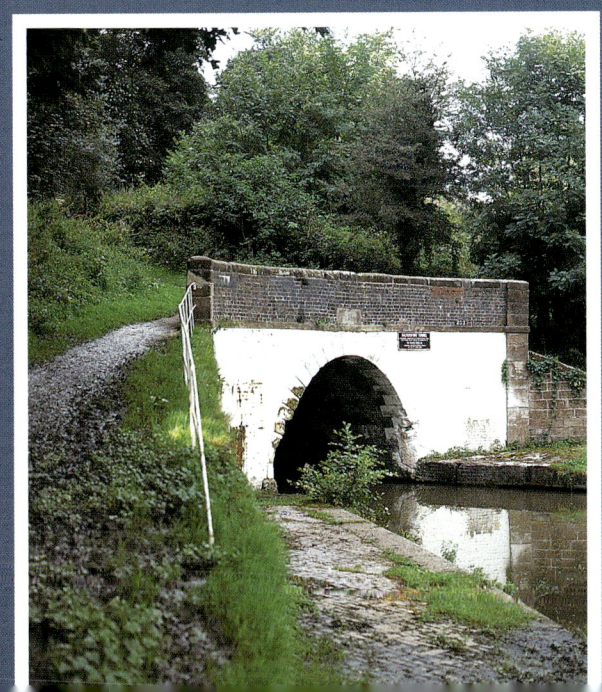

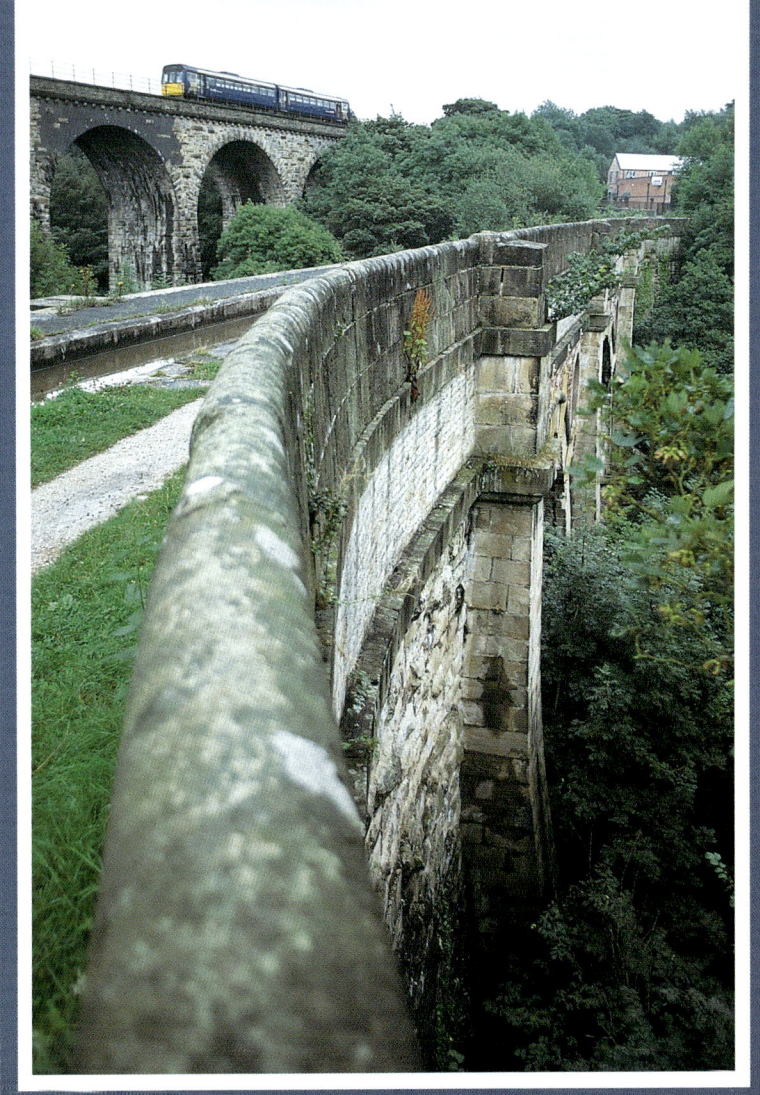

Further south along the Trent & Mersey Canal lies **Harecastle Tunnel**. All of 2,897 yards in length, it is necessary to employ a system of forced ventilation to deal with the diesel fumes made by boats passing through it. There is no room for boats to pass inside and so entries operate to a strict timetable and tunnel-keepers monitor the progress of each boat. A smart office and shower block has been built at the northern *(above)* end of the tunnel, whilst the southern *(right)* portal is equipped with doors and also houses the extractor fans. Note the curious orange colour of the canal water, caused by tiny particles of ironstone seeping out from underground springs in the vicinity. Incidentally, it takes boats around three-quarters of an hour to negotiate the tunnel, truly an adventure, though not for the faint-hearted.

Still in North Staffordshire, but in telling contrast to the length and strategic importance of Harecastle Tunnel, **Leek Tunnel** *(left)* lies virtually at the end of the Leek Branch of the Caldon Canal, a remote backwater even by canal standards, but well worth seeking out, perhaps as part of an exploration of the canal scene at Hazelhurst Junction and a visit to Cheddleton Flint Mill.

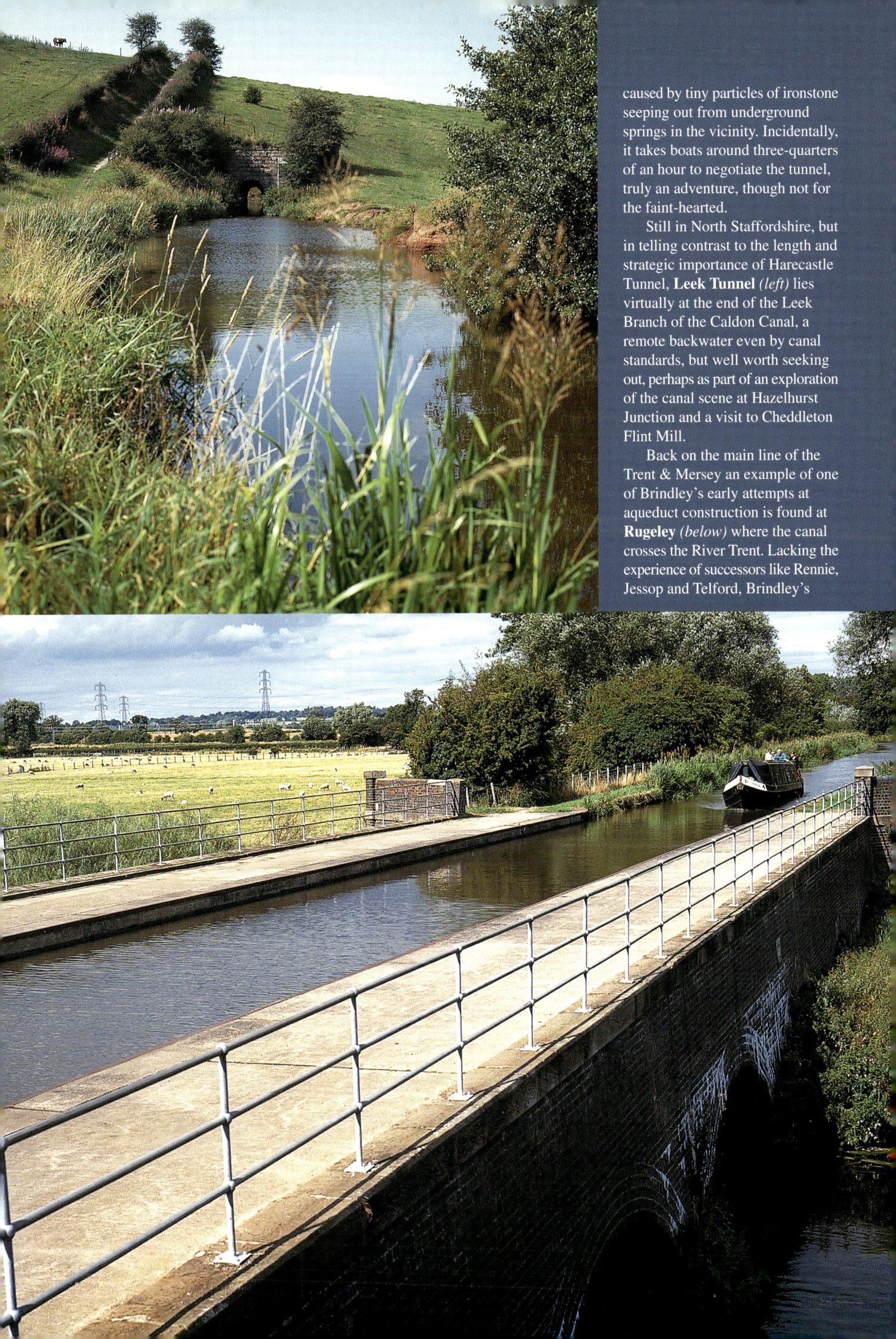

Back on the main line of the Trent & Mersey an example of one of Brindley's early attempts at aqueduct construction is found at **Rugeley** *(below)* where the canal crosses the River Trent. Lacking the experience of successors like Rennie, Jessop and Telford, Brindley's aqueducts were largely low-slung affairs, sturdy masonry arches carrying the canal in its traditional bed of puddled-clay. Another example of this tentative approach can be found on the Montgomery Canal *(above)* where it crosses the River Vyrnwy near **Llanymynech**, south-west of Oswestry. This stretch of the Montgomery Canal has yet to be restored to navigation, but you can walk across the aqueduct or get a good view of it from the neighbouring road bridge over the river.

Not all canal tunnels are quite what you'd expect them to be. The 'tunnel' pictured *(right)* was provided to take a by-road beneath the giant Shelmore Embankment near **Norbury Junction**. Cautious driving is advisable, but this - and the corresponding underpass at the Gnosall end of the bank - repay the effort of finding a quiet spot to park on the verge.

A little bit further south, the Shropshire Union Canal - originally known as the Birmingham & Liverpool Junction Canal - crosses the A5 on an exquisite little aqueduct at **Stretton**. This view *(below)* shows the delightful cast iron balustrade on the aqueduct's wing wall, with the road below and the canal stretching towards Brewood at the top right hand corner.

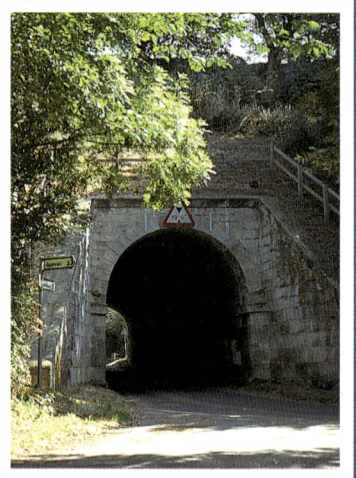

Stretton Aqueduct was designed by Thomas Telford. Another famous Scottish engineer, John Rennie, lays claim to three of the country's most gracious aqueducts: **Dundas** *(above)* and Avoncliff on the Kennet & Avon Canal, and the **Lune Aqueduct** *(right)* which carries the Lancaster Canal over the River Lune on the northern outskirts of Lancaster. Dundas Aqueduct takes the Kennet & Avon Canal across the River Avon a few miles east of Bath. It was completed in 1805 and named after the first chairman of the canal, Charles Dundas. The Lune Aqueduct dates from 1797. Next time you're on the M6, turn off at Junction 34 and spare a few minutes to admire it in all its glory.

Scheduled Flights & Early Risers

LOCKS are the most defining canal structures and well-known 'flights' or groups of them attract many land-based visitors every year. One of the most famous and visually dramatic flights in the country is the **Caen Hill** Flight of locks *(above)* on the Kennet & Avon Canal near Devizes. It's one of the 'Seven Wonders of the Waterways' and its sixteen chambers are part of a group of twenty-nine locks which lift the canal by 237 feet in two miles. In Devizes itself you can visit the excellent Kennet & Avon Trust's shop and museum. A few miles west along the same canal, **Seend Locks** *(below)* are altogether quieter and less-visited, though there is a well-frequented pub called the Barge Inn nearby!

For all their inherent variety, canal locks can largely be divided into two main types: narrow and wide. At about seven feet wide and seventy feet in length, the traditional narrow lock characterises many of the canals of the midlands and north-west which form the most popular holiday cruising routes. Pictured here *(above left)* on the Caldon Canal at **Hazelhurst Junction** is a typical narrow lock, whilst *(above right)* is a wide lock on the Trent & Mersey Canal at **Stenson** capable of accepting two narrowbeam boats side by side. A fascinating 'figure of eight' walk can be enjoyed based on Deep Hayes Country Park near Leek in the vicinity of Hazelhurst Junction. Stenson, on the outskirts of Derby, is also easily accessible and visitor numbers are boosted by the presence of a popular pub.

On the picturesque Staffordshire & Worcestershire Canal at **The Bratch** *(below)* a flight of three closely spaced locks gives the appearance of a staircase or riser, but in fact these are three conventional lock chambers squeezed together with extensive side ponds which add to the interest of the location where a car park and picnic site has been provided to encourage visitors. Because boats cannot pass in the flight, a lock keeper is usually on hand to ensure smooth operation and no fraying of tempers amongst the boat crews, who have to exercise patience, particularly in the high season when sizeable queues can occur.

To overcome problems of congestion when the canals were at their most successful, and often overwhelmed by the sheer volume of cargoes being carried, some locks were duplicated

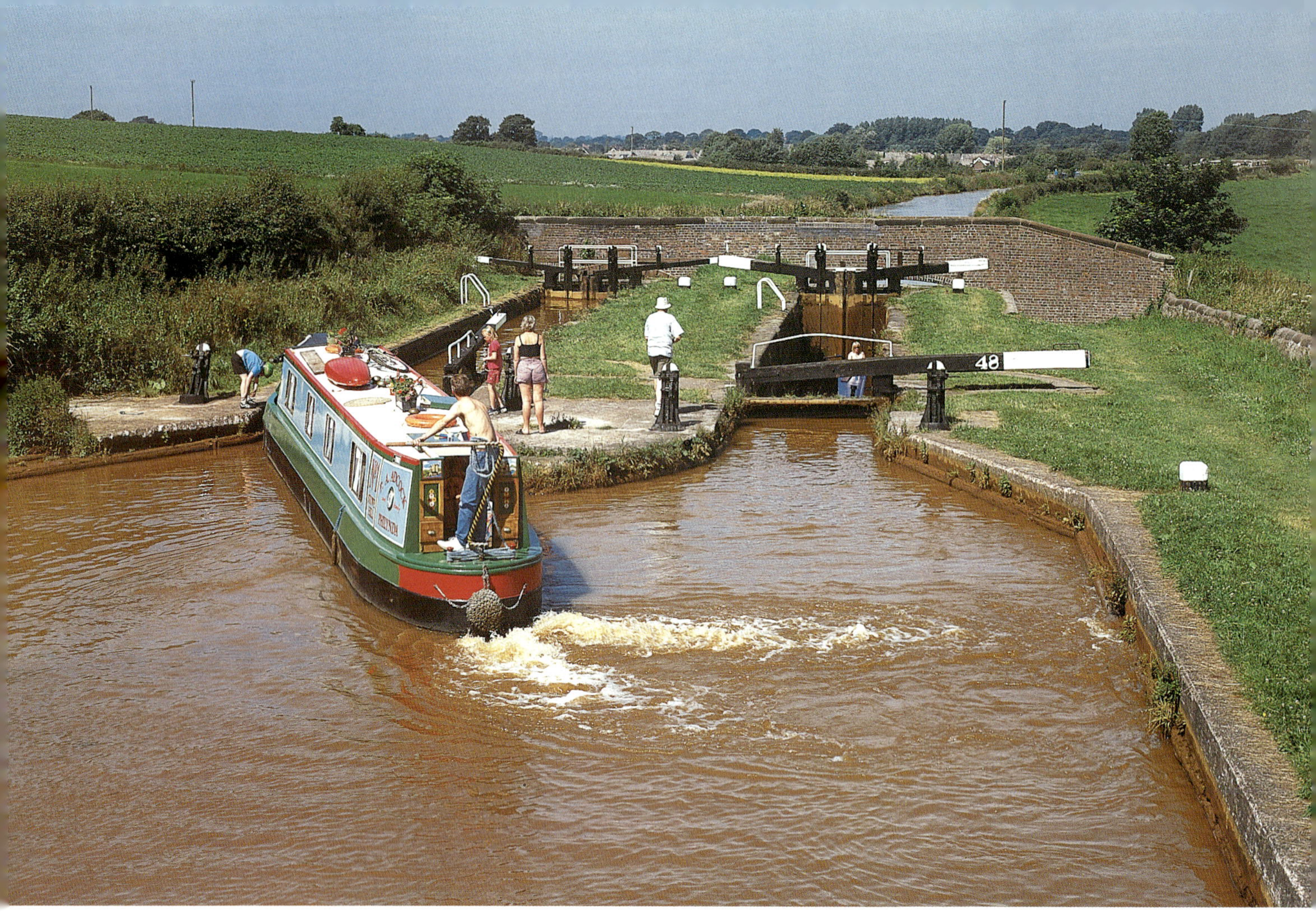
48

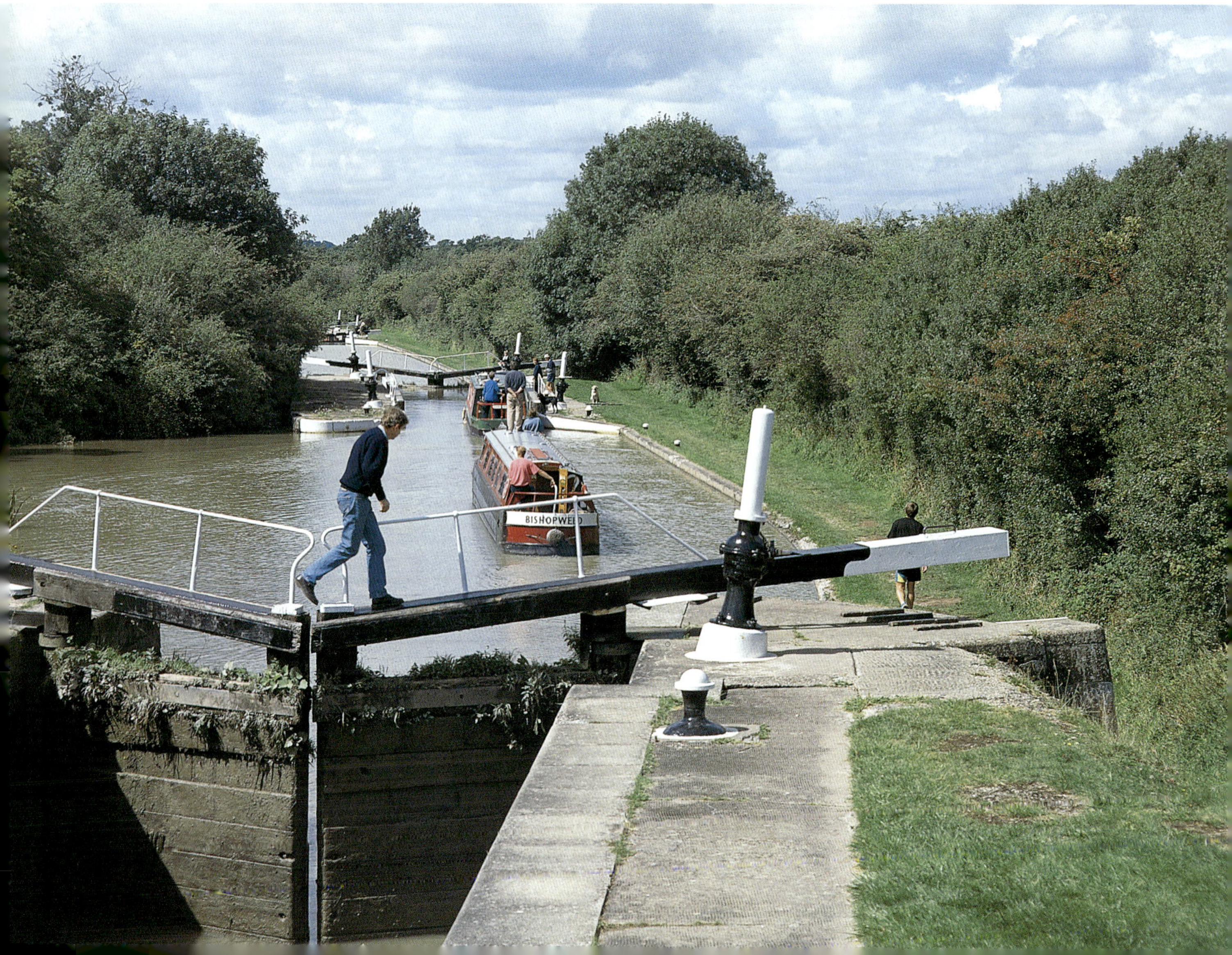

to ease the flow of boat traffic. The Trent & Mersey Canal has examples of this between Kidsgrove and Middlewich as seen here *(opposite upper)* at **Church Locks** where modern-day leisure-boaters find the duplication equally useful. Church Locks are part of 'Heartbreak Hill', a daunting sequence of twenty-six locks in seven miles facing boaters climbing out of the Cheshire Plain into the foothills of North Staffordshire.

Wide locks can also be handy in speeding up present day boat movements. Indeed, British Waterways encourage the sharing of locks to conserve water supplies. The **Grand Union Canal** between Napton and Knowle in Warwickshire *(opposite lower)* features flights of locks widened in the 1930s in the sadly unrealised hope that wide barges might be introduced to trade between London and Birmingham.

The Grand Union network, formed in 1929 by amalgamation, features many interesting lock flights, as *(above left)* at **Watford** in Northamptonshire where in a flight of seven narrow chambers there is a dramatic staircase of four which draws its water supplies from massive side ponds. Back on the main line of the Grand Union is **Stocker's Lock** *(above right)* to the south of Rickmansworth, from which point regular boat trips operate. Note the quaint lock-keeper's cottage and its lovely garden.

Braunston Bottom Lock - framed between a popular canal gift shop and a handsome covered drydock - is also on the Grand Union Canal. In this picture *(right)* two holiday narrowboats are sharing the chamber while the lock is being emptied. When the water levels equate, the gates can be swung open to let the two boats out on to the lower level of the canal - simple!

Further up the Grand Union's Leicester Section the canal joins the River Soar. **Cossington Lock** *(above)* is typical of those to be found on this navigation, and though alongside a busy section of the A6, lies in a peaceful setting of watermeadows. Nearby is the village of Rothley which has a station on the preserved Great Central Railway.

The northernmost section of the Grand Union empire was the Erewash Canal. Its locks are widebeam too as here *(left)* at **Sandiacre** just short of the junction with the former Derby Canal between the East Midland towns of Long Eaton and Ilkeston. The lock-keeper's cottage is dated 1779 and has been taken over by local enthusiasts who open its interesting doors to the public on Sunday afternoons. The Erewash Canal is something of a backwater nowadays, though it would undoubtedly have been more popular with boaters had its connection with the highly scenic Cromford Canal to the north remained intact.

A rival route to the Grand Union between the midlands and London is the Oxford Canal. It locks have always remained narrow and most of its trade disappeared long before that on the Grand Union. Mostly rural in character, and highly picturesque in its wanderings through the Cherwell Valley, it is one of the most popular holiday boating canals.

Somerton Lock *(above)* illustrates just how pretty the Oxford Canal can be. With a twelve foot rise/fall it is one of the deepest narrow chambers on the canal network. In working boat days it was the habit of boat captains engaged in the coal trade down to Morrells Brewery at Oxford to exchange lumps of coal for fresh laid eggs and locally trapped rabbits. **Aynho Weir Lock** *(right)*, the next lock north along the canal, was constructed to an unusual diamond shape to compensate for the extreme depth of Somerton.

Banbury is the only town of any size on the Oxford Canal between Oxford and the outskirts of Coventry. Up until the 1950s a canal community centered around Tooley's Dock which you can read about in L.T.C. Rolt's classic canal book *Narrow Boat*. The canalscape at **Banbury Lock** *(left)* has changed a great deal in recent times with the construction of a new shopping centre, but there is a good deal of canal tradition and heritage still associated with the town and this is reflected in the new Banbury Museum adjacent to the canal. The railway station is handily placed nearby.

Up North canal locks are generally of larger dimensions than their midland brethren, reflecting the texture of the Pennine landscape they occupy. The two views on this page are of locks on the Rochdale Canal restored to full navigable status as a Trans-Pennine canal in 2002, a hundred and ninety-eight years after its completion. The Rochdale boasts no less than ninety-two locks in just thirty-two miles, which perhaps explains why it has yet to attract large numbers of boaters!

Gauxholme Locks *(above)* are located just south-west of the town of Todmorden. They are part of a fascinating section of canal as it climbs from its eastern extremity at Sowerby Bridge to its short summit, six hundred feet above sea level. Note the imposingly Gothic railway bridge which spans the flight. You only have to follow the towpath for the short distance between Todmorden to Walsden railway stations to experience the unique atmosphere of the Rochdale Canal.

At the other end of the summit, **Summit Locks** *(left)* mark the beginning of the canal's descent towards Manchester, nineteen miles away. The boat in the picture is making its way eastwards

The Calder & Hebble Navigation is a characterful, yet comparatively little known waterway which prods its finger up from the rhubarb growing fields of Wakefield towards the post-industrial woollen mill towns of the West Riding. Its locks are broad and accompanied by unusual operating mechanisms. Pictured *(above)* are **Thornhill Double Locks** on the outskirts of Dewsbury. Also in the West Riding, but much better known, is the famous **Bingley Five Rise** *(right)* which Robert Aickman, founder of the Inland Waterways Association, designated as one of the Severn Wonders of the Waterways. The five massive staircase locks lift the canal some sixty feet and can easily be seen as part of a short walk between the railway stations of Bingley and Crossflatts served by frequent trains. Further temptation to visit the 5 rise comes from its proximity to Damart's woollen underwear factory shop.

Function @ The Junction

WHERE a motorway interchange would spread in ungainly style over an acre or two of land, a meeting of canals is usually achieved in the simplest of circumstances, a simple (and usually beautiful) bridge spanning the confluence of the two routes to facilitate the passage of boat horses from one side to the other. There is no finer an example of this simplicity than at **Great Haywood** *(above)* where the Staffordshire & Worcestershire Canal sets off on its 46 mile journey to the River Severn from the Trent & Mersey Canal. The flatness of its arch is reminiscent of Brunel's railway bridge across the Thames at Maidenhead; though Brindley's bridge is the senior by over seventy years, and therefore perhaps the more daring. Further along the Staffs & Worcs - surely one of the prettiest canals - the inland navigator comes upon **Stourton Junction** *(right)* where the canal to

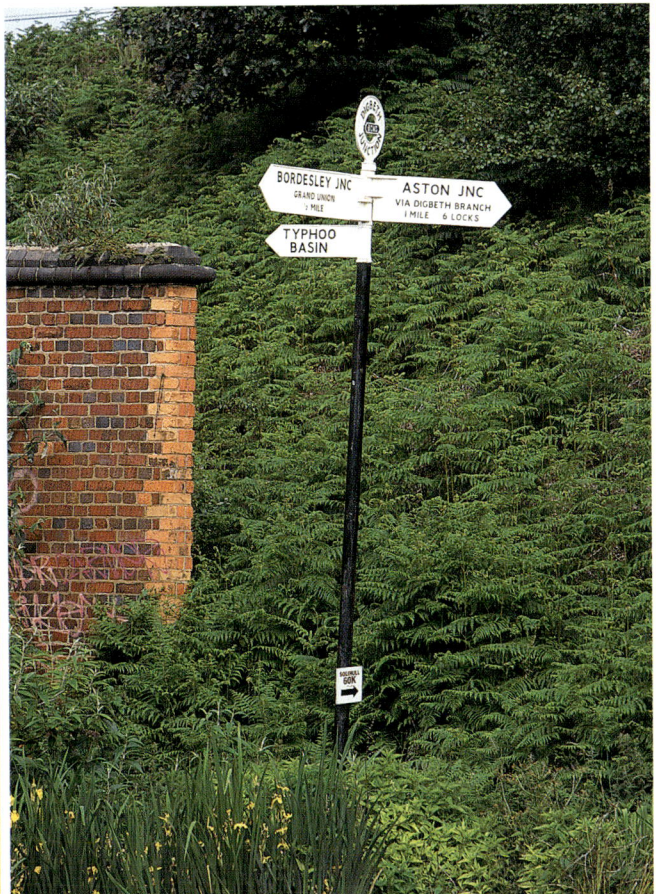

Stourbridge diverges from the Staffordshire & Worcestershire Canal. On the frayed hem of the West Midlands conurbation, the two canals meet in what is perhaps the first area of true countryside west of Coventry. A few hundred yards south of the junction lies Stewponey Wharf and an interesting group of former canal workshops, plus a toll house intriguingly now operated as a gift shop by a fortune-teller.

Being at its densest, the canal network of the midlands features many junctions. Should you follow the Stourbridge Canal up from Stourton Junction you'll come upon the Dudley Canals, part of the famous Birmingham Canal Navigations system which once amounted to 160 route miles. **Windmill End** *(above)* is one of the best-known locations on the Dudley No.2 Canal, a highly photogenic grouping of typical BCN junction bridges overlooked by the gaunt silhouette of an old engine house, the sort of post-industrial landmark more commonly associated with the Cornish tin industry. These cast iron 'roving' bridges, variously built at Toll End or Horseley, remain one of the most potent images of the Black Country's canals, marking the bifurcation of many a junction and egress of many an arm. Invariably, in junction locations, they are accompanied by signposts of the sort pictured *(left)* at **Digbeth** close to the heart of Birmingham itself.

Approximately a hundred miles of the Birmingham Canal Navigations remain navigable, and whilst all of this fascinating network doesn't necessarily attract boating holidaymakers in large numbers, sometimes the more popular cruising lengths, such as the main line between Birmingham and Wolverhampton - an integral part of two 'rings' - provides startlingly surreal images, such as that *(above)* at **Rotton Park Junction** where the Icknield Port and Soho loops, which originally formed Brindley's contour-clinging route between the two towns, are crossed by Telford's more direct main line. Some of the trip-boats operating out of Brindley Place and the International Convention Centre include these loops in their itineraries, and they can provide an entertaining introduction to the secret world of the canals on Birmingham's 21st century doorstep.

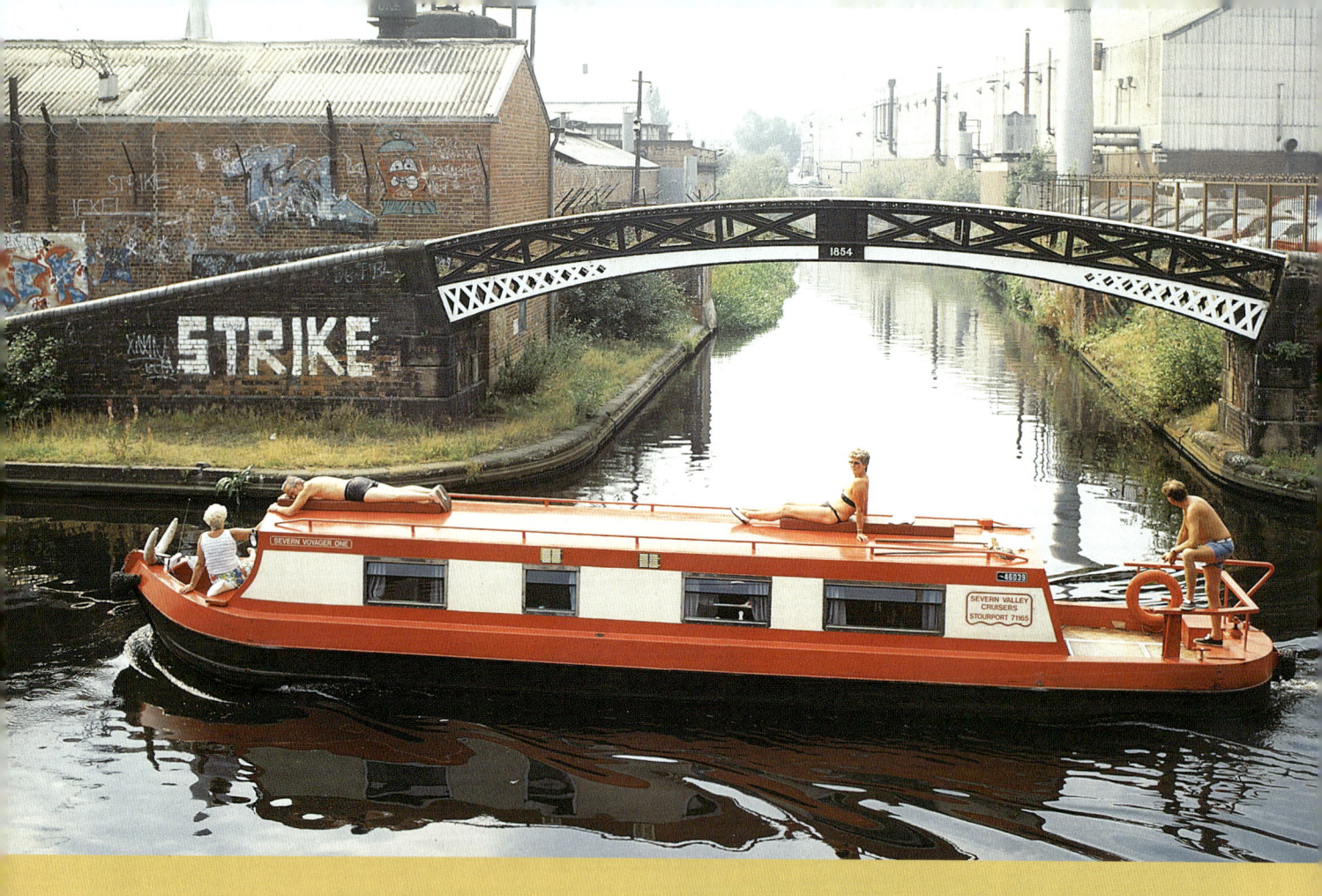

A similar scene can be found at **Deepfields Junction**, near Coseley, where another truncated section of the original main line goes wandering off into a world of wastegrounds and tethered ponies, though at this location *(right)* a modern access road provides a contrasting 20th century intrusion in concrete, and it is hard to believe that in two hundred years time anyone will go out of their way to visit this.

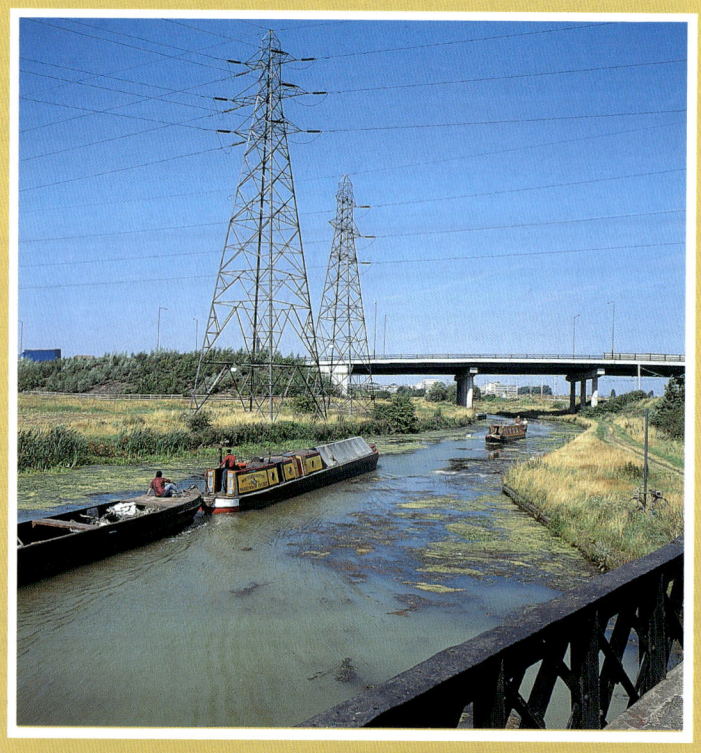

The Birmingham & Fazeley Canal sets off from the 'Second City' in a roughly easterly direction to form a junction with the Coventry Canal at **Fazeley**, near Tamworth, where British Waterways have established their regional headquarters. The junction of the two canals - seen *(left)* through the arch of a bridge carrying the A5 London-Holyhead road - is overlooked by a graceful junction house typical of the innate, bricks & mortar dignity which you encounter time and time again on the canals. Turn left and you can make your way to the Trent & Mersey Canal at Fradley. Turn right, and you can proceed at a steady three miles an hour all the way to London, 145 miles away.

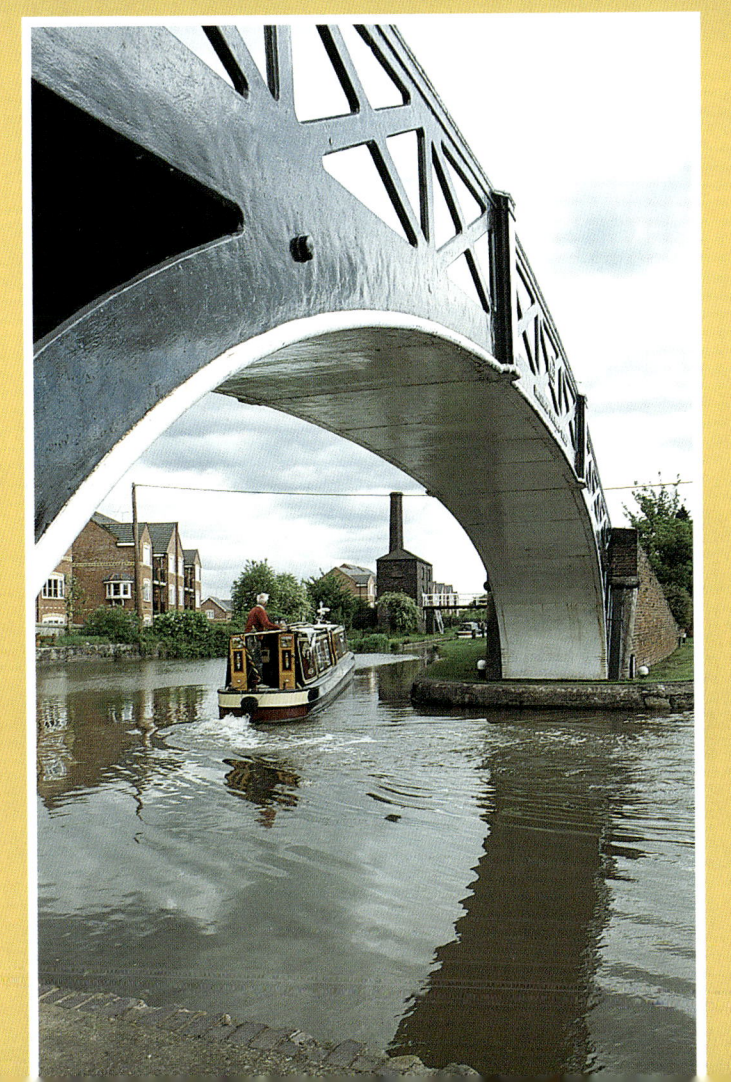

At the northern end of the Coventry Canal lies **Fradley Junction**, near Lichfield, immensely popular with motorists, lured by both the attractiveness of the location and the convivial Swan Inn seen here *(above)* with its grandstand view, at the meeting of the two canals, looking directly southwards towards the Coventry Canal as a narrow boat makes its way through the locks on the Trent & Mersey Canal in the direction of Stoke-on-Trent.

At the other end of the Coventry Canal - a vital link between the canals of the north and the south - is **Hawkesbury Junction** *(left)* on the outskirts of Coventry, where boaters are faced with a tight U turn to make their way between the Coventry Canal and the Oxford Canal. Ideally all their attention is demanded by the tightness of the bend, but few will not want to pay at least some respect to the wonderful cast iron bridge which spans the entrance to the Oxford Canal. Clearly emblazoned on the centre of its impressive arch is the date and place of its origin: 1837, Britannia Foundry, Derby.

In the vernacular of working boatmen and their families, Hawkesbury was known colloquially as 'Sutton Stop'. Boats would congregate here at the edge of the Warwickshire coalfield, awaiting orders to load at neighbouring pits. Another well known canalside pub catered for their prodigious thirst. Go to Hawkesbury now and you can still enjoy a pint at The Greyhound; though, sadly, boaters dancing on the table tops to the strains of an accordion are unlikely to disturb your peace. The tall-chimnied building to the rear of the bridge in the picture is a former pumping engine house.

Irrespective of whether they are in rural locations as *(above)* at **Gayton** on the Grand Union Canal where the Northampton Arm begins its descent to the County Town and River Nene, or industrial as *(below)* at **Water's Meeting** on the western outskirts of Manchester, canal junctions have a peculiarly self-contained feel to them which can make them difficult to locate by road. Also, it bears remembering that not all junctions are still technically 'junctions' at all where one or other of the routes has been abandoned. Naturally there is a melancholy sense of loss about such locations as you contemplate journeys which may no longer be made, not afloat at any rate. At **Shipley** in West Yorkshire *(above)* only the shortest of stubs remains within a lugubrious landscape of mills where the Bradford Canal once egressed from the Leeds & Liverpool. Similarly, little more than an arm is still in water at **Norbury Junction** *(left)* in Staffordshire where the Newport Branch of the Shropshire Union Canal once departed from the main line on its way to Shrewsbury. Unfortunately, campaigns to have this route restored have, as yet, not come to fruition, though Norbury Junction itself is a popular canal location with a British Waterways office and maintenance yard, a hire base and a pub.

Working Boats

CANALS, of course, were built with the business of carrying cargoes in mind - the leisure industry which dominates them now cannot possibly have been forseen by the system's 18th century promoters. Sadly, comparatively little freight is carried by water now, and most of that is centered on Yorkshire, on the widebeam navigations which radiate from the River Humber. Typical traffics now are aggregates and petroleum, and Castleford, between Wakefield and Leeds is perhaps one of the best places to go and look for *real* barges! The two views *(opposite)* were taken on the Aire & Calder Navigation near **Woodlesford**. *Eskdale* was built as a tanker barge for a now defunct, but once well-known, company called Harkers, but nowadays it is mostly engaged in carrying sand between the River Trent and West Yorkshire.

On the narrow-beam, midland canals, commercial trade is to all intents and purposes obsolete, but a number of determined enthusiasts eke out an archaic existence carrying domestic coal around the system which they retail direct from the boat to their customers. One such narrowboat can be seen in this picture *(below)* running the gauntlet of anglers on the Trent & Mersey Canal near **Middlewich**. From time to time new initiatives emerge to bring back cargo-carrying to the narrow canals, but sadly they almost inevitably flounder in the face of bureaucracy and road competition.

Canines on cabin tops! A gloriously restored Cowburn & Cowpar butty - crewed by an equally attractive young steerer - is seen *(above)* waiting to enter the single, narrowbeam lock at **Wheaton Aston** on the Shropshire Union Canal, its powered motor having preceeded it into the chamber.

Gas Street Basin in **Birmingham** *(below)* is usually a location which can be counted on to produce examples of traditional working craft. Whilst not replicating a traditional livery as such, this brightly painted boat keeps to the spirit of things - the dog obviously approves!

Thankfully, many examples of working boats have been preserved at centres accessible by the general public. Sometimes this is achieved on a modest scale as *(above)* at **Rickmansworth** on the Grand Union Canal where a small interpretation centre informs visitors as to the history of waterways in the area and offers the chance to inspect this delightfully restored Harvey-Taylor boat which was actually built nearby.

Altogether more ambitious in outlook is the Boat Museum *(below)* at **Ellesmere Port** in Cheshire where numerous craft from a wide variety of canals and river navigations have been brought together in the atmospheric setting of a once major port of transhipment.

REGISTERED AT RICKMANSWORTH No23
PRINCE
ASSOCIATED CANAL CARRIERS LTD
LONDON & NORTHAMPTON

DARWEN
REG No 1744
BRITISH WATERWAYS
LIVERPOOL

Many traditional working craft have been preserved privately by groups or individuals, the equivalent, perhaps, of traction engines or classic cars. From time to time, in amongst all the pleasure craft, you come upon them quite by chance, making their way to or from a rally maybe, or simply moored up. Such encounters add colour to your own personal canal scene and can be the highlight of a holiday afloat.

The narrowboat *Prince* is seen *(opposite upper)* working its way up the **Walsall** Flight, whilst the Leeds & Liverpool shortboat *Darwen* is moored by Trencherfield Mill *(opposite lower)* **Wigan**. A pair of boats in British Waterways blue & yellow livery is pictured *(above)* at Castlefield, **Manchester**, whilst, finally, the proud bow of *Columba* is seen *(right)* moored at **Stoke Bruerne**.

Wharves & Warehouses

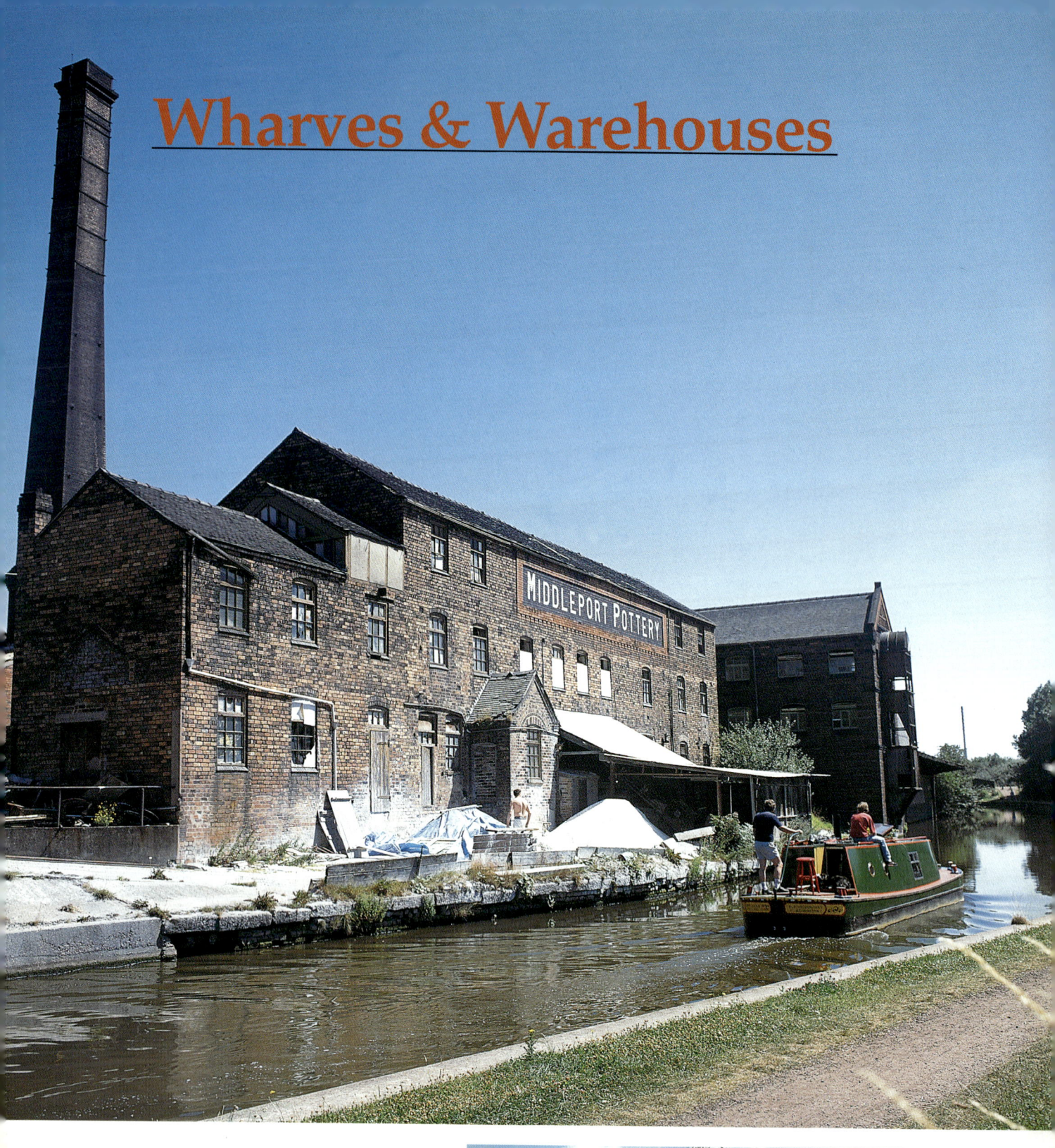

It is not that many years ago - say forty to forty-five - that working boats were still bringing cargoes of china clay down from the Mersey ports along the Trent & Mersey Canal to the pottery wharves of Burslem and Stoke in North Staffordshire. Many of these highly characterful works survive - as *(above)* at **Middleport** - but now their raw materials are brought in for the most part by road, although there are also regular consignments of china clay railed in from Cornwall, which at least eradicates some lorry movements along the M5 and M6 motorways.

But most canal wharves in this country - even if their adjacent industrial premises are still very much in business - lie disconcertingly moribund as is the case *(right)* at **Chillington Wharf** on the outskirts of Wolverhampton, once a hive of activity where canal boats and railway wagons would exchange cargoes for onward consignment via each respective mode of transport. Some sense of lost activity is engendered at Chillington Wharf by the fact that its railway tracks remain in use for the storage of steel wagons. But the canal water is reedy and silted as you can see, and life is lent to the vicinity nowadays not by the passage of working boats but by the passage of modern trams on the adjacent Bilston road.

Wolverhampton itself is a fascinating canal centre, its famous flight of twenty-one locks being well worth the energy expended in working them! Frustratingly, many of its former canal warehouses have been bulldozed into oblivion, when, given better luck, new uses might have been more effectively found for them. One survivor, however, is the **Albion Wharf** *(above)*, now finding itself in peaceful, leafy surroundings whereas, in the past, these oily, clouded waters would have been thronged with boats loading and unloading whilst others impatiently attempted to batter their way through the throng.

There were town wharves and there were village wharves, as exemplified by **Lower Heyford** on the Oxford Canal *(below)*. Now in use as a holiday hire base, it would once have served neighbouring villages in the Cherwell Valley, exporting locally grown agricultural produce and importing the benefits of civilisation, or what passed for them: coal, building materials, early forms of machinery. Commercially, it would have thrived until the railway came, Brunel's Great Western thrusting its way up from Oxford to Banbury. Nowadays, this is perhaps a rare example of canal wharf and country station surviving side by side: the wharf as a busy and successful boatyard for leisure craft, the station as a railhead for commuters; Paddington is only 85 minutes away. The Oxford Canal is one of the most popular cruising routes, and although villages like Lower Heyford have lost their shops to competition from supermarkets, the village pub continues to flourish, a good degree of its trade emanating from the canal, walkers and boaters alike.

It is not only villages that derive a good deal of extra income from canal trade. Sizeable country towns like **Market Drayton** *(overleaf upper)* and **Market Harborough** *(overleaf lower)* also benefit hugely from the presence of a canal on their doorstep. The Shropshire Union Canal runs from Wolverhampton to Ellesmere Port on the banks of the River Mersey, and Market Drayton is one of just three settlements of any size encountered en route. In its case the warehouse which graced its wharf was used for the storage of cheese, an important commodity in this dairy farming district. Now it houses a gift shop, a cafe and boatyard premises, appropriate uses for an attractive building which would otherwise have lain derelict or suffered demolition.

Market Harborough lies at the end of an arm off the Leicester Section of the Grand Union Canal. The wharf had

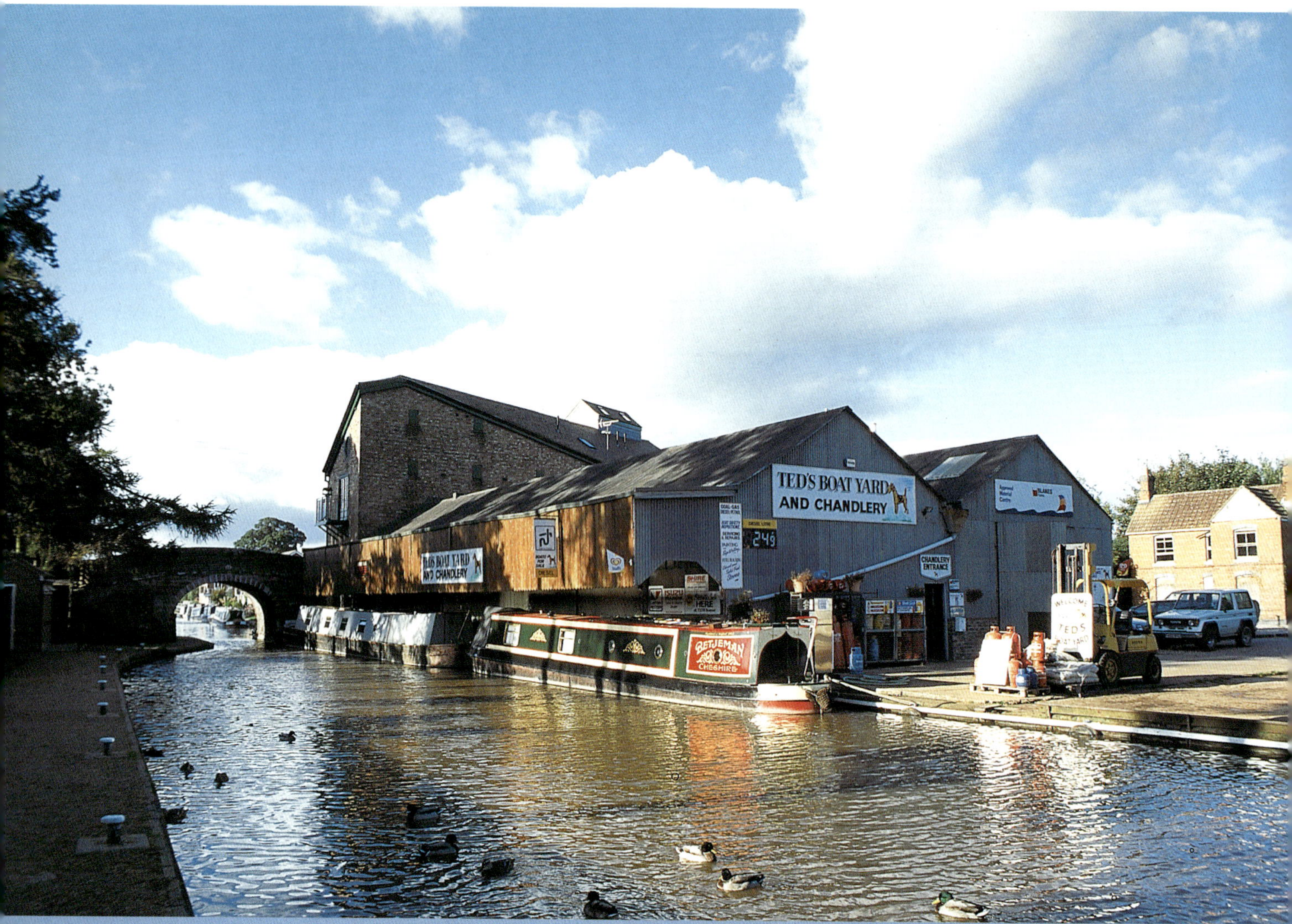
TED'S BOAT YARD
AND CHANDLERY

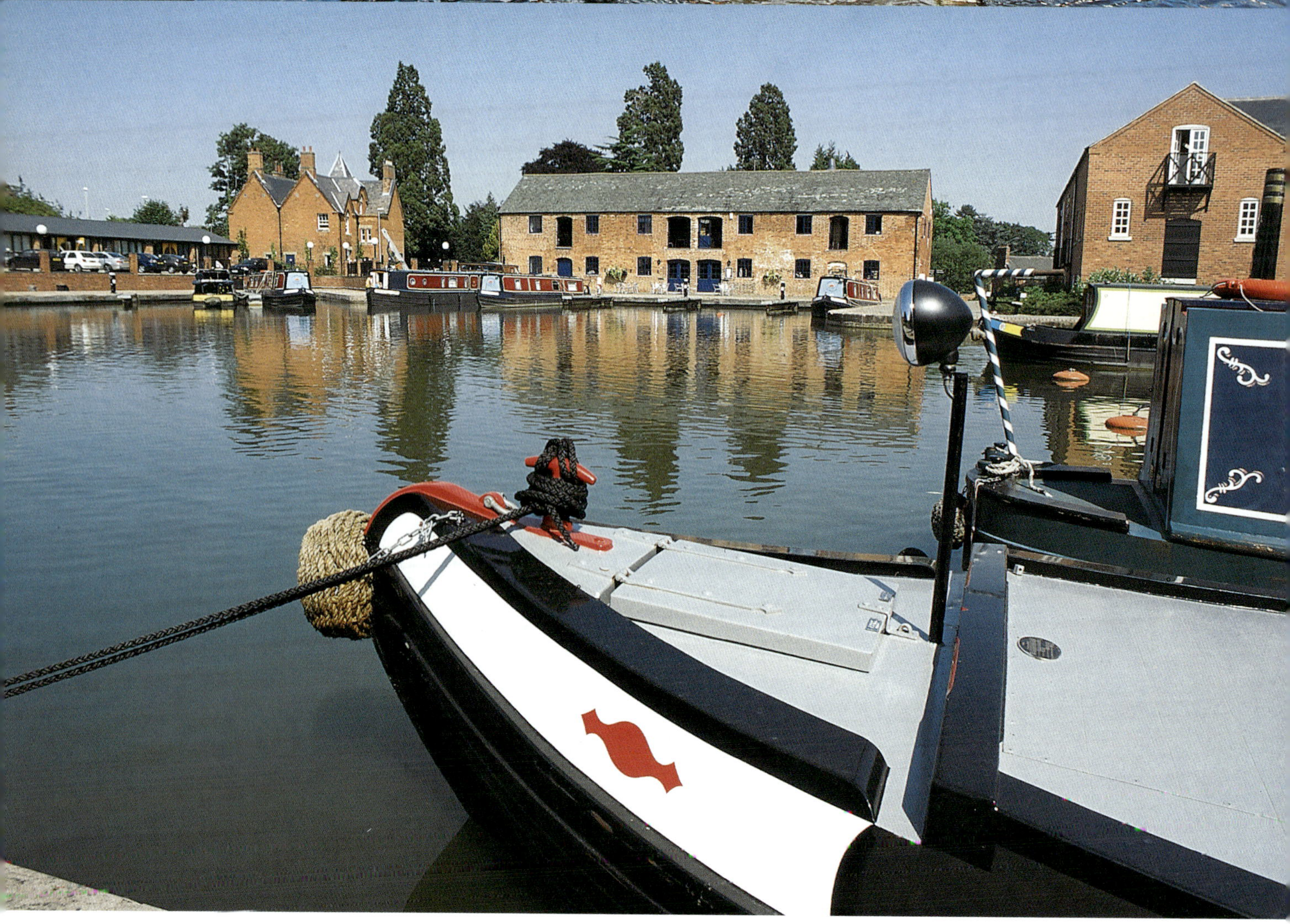

lain largely derelict for a number of years before a multi-million pound facelift transformed its fortune. Now it is home to a time-share fleet and a very attractive Italian restaurant whose tables spill out on to the quayside on warm days, just the place to watch the waterways world go by! In 1950 the terminal basin was the scene of the Inland Waterway Association's very first festival.

Campaigning by the IWA and other interested bodies is resulting in the revival of another canal on the opposite side of the midlands - in fact in Wales - the Montgomery Canal. Following a breach in 1936, it lay derelict for over half a century until canal enthusiasts began to restore lengths of it piecemeal in the 1980s. Now two lengthy sections of it can be boated once again and work on the missing sections continues as funding permits. At **Welshpool** *(above)* the former warehouse has found new use as a museum of local heritage, and boats are available for hire by the day or longer for exploration of a twelve mile section of the Montgomery Canal between Arddleen and Berriew through some of the most beautiful countryside in the Welsh Marches.

Better known, even still, are the canal museums at **Gloucester Docks** *(right upper)* and **Stoke Bruerne** *(right lower)* in Northamptonshire. The former is officially designated the National Waterways Museum, but the latter is the senior, dating from 1963, and formed out of the collection of the local lock-keeper. Gloucester Docks lie at the landward end of the Gloucester & Sharpness Canal, built to facilitate the movement of ships between the Severn estuary and Gloucester, an inland port of commercial significance until the 1980s. Gloucester docks became well known subliminally to millions of television viewers in the late 1970s as a backdrop to the television series *The Onedin Line*. Stoke Bruerne is on the Grand Union Canal at the southern end of Blisworth Tunnel. An unspoilt Northamptonshire village, picturesque in its own right, never mind the canal, it attracts tens of thousands of visitors each year, the personification of middle England.

As you travel around the inland waterways system, you will inevitably come upon former warehouses which have experienced mixed fortunes during the leisure age. Regeneration is to be welcomed - well usually! - though paradoxically it is often the warehouses which have been abandoned to a slow decay that retain a more redolent atmosphere of the past.

Being refurbished into pubs and restaurants is a fate that has occurred to many warehouses, and it is usually an enjoyable experience to dine or drink in such surroundings. Examples of this are pictured *(above)* at the old inland port of **Shardlow** near Derby, where the substantial and handsome Clock Warehouse is enjoying a second new lease of life, having previously been refurbished as a canal museum. The Orwell *(below left)* at **Wigan** is another example of a warehouse being transformed into a popular watering hole, part of the Wigan Pier heritage centre.

Warehouses yet to be redeveloped include this one *(below right)* at **Wakefield** on the Calder & Hebble Navigation or *(opposite upper)* Lord Talbot's Wharf on an isolated section of the Shropshire Union Canal north of **Wheaton Aston**.

Sometimes you can find a new and appropriate use for a former warehouse without being too brash about it as at **Froghall** *(opposite lower)* on the Caldon Canal where you can buy ice creams and simply soak up the old magic of a wharf area which was once anything but quiet and peaceful.

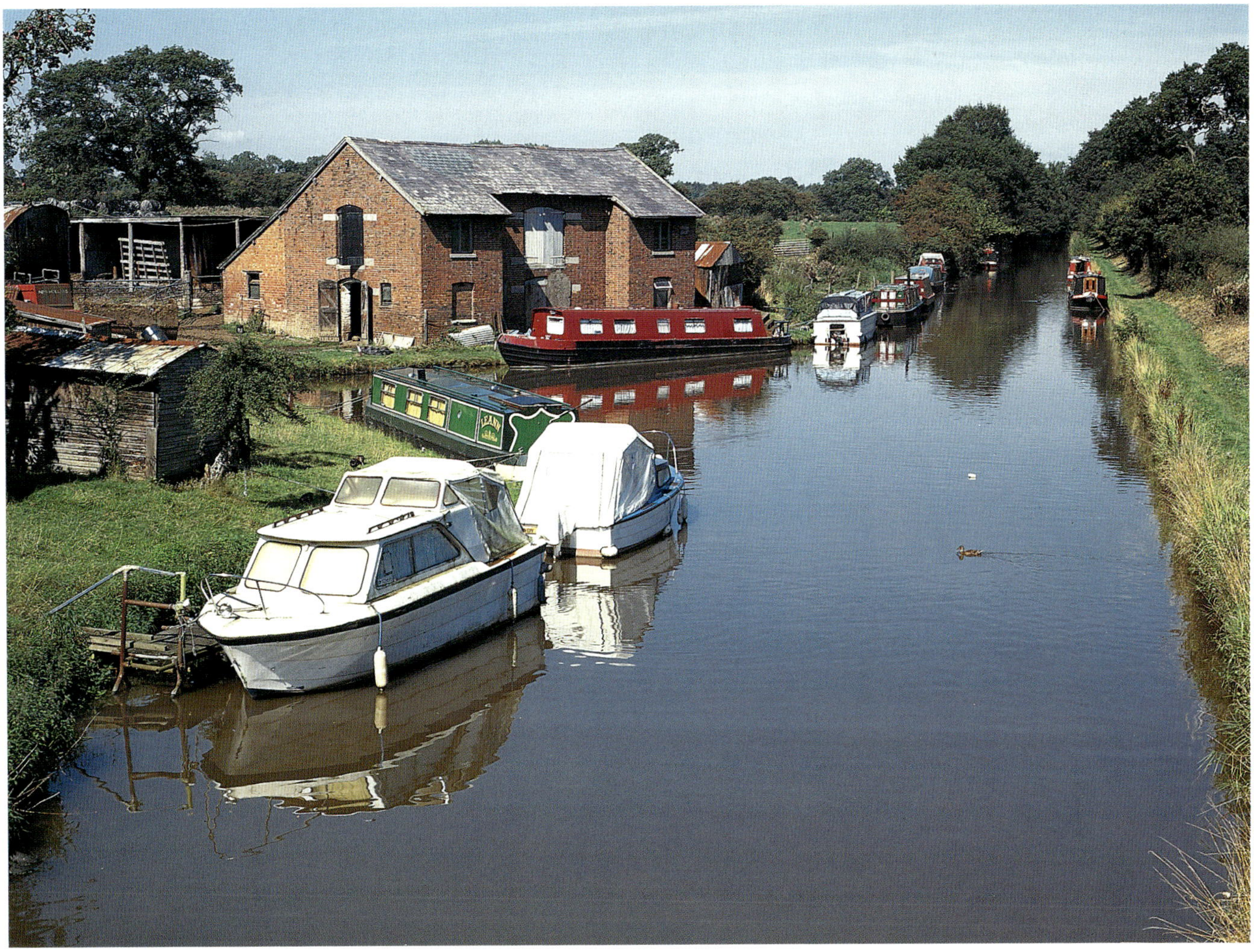

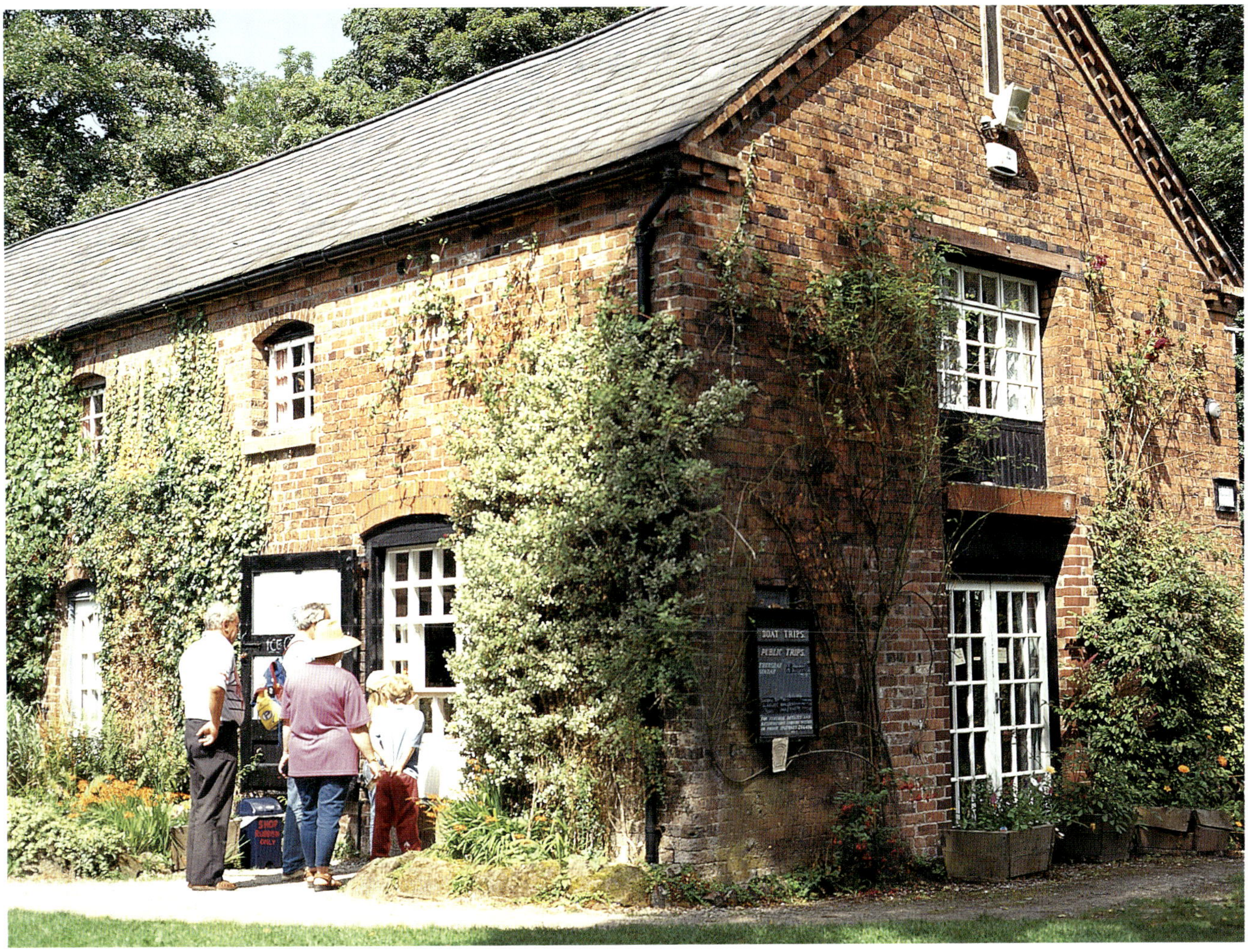
BOAT TRIPS
PUBLIC TRIPS

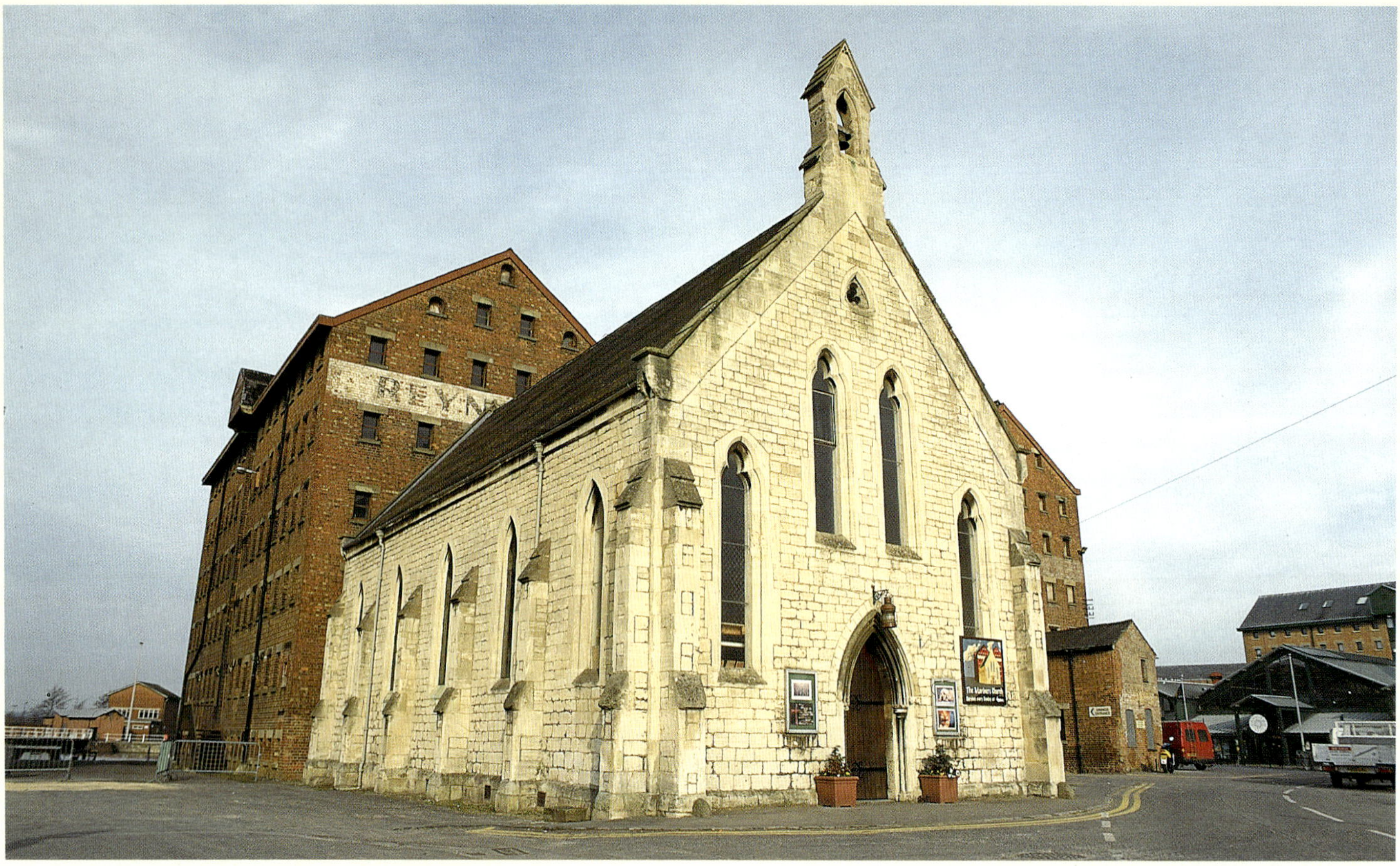
REYN

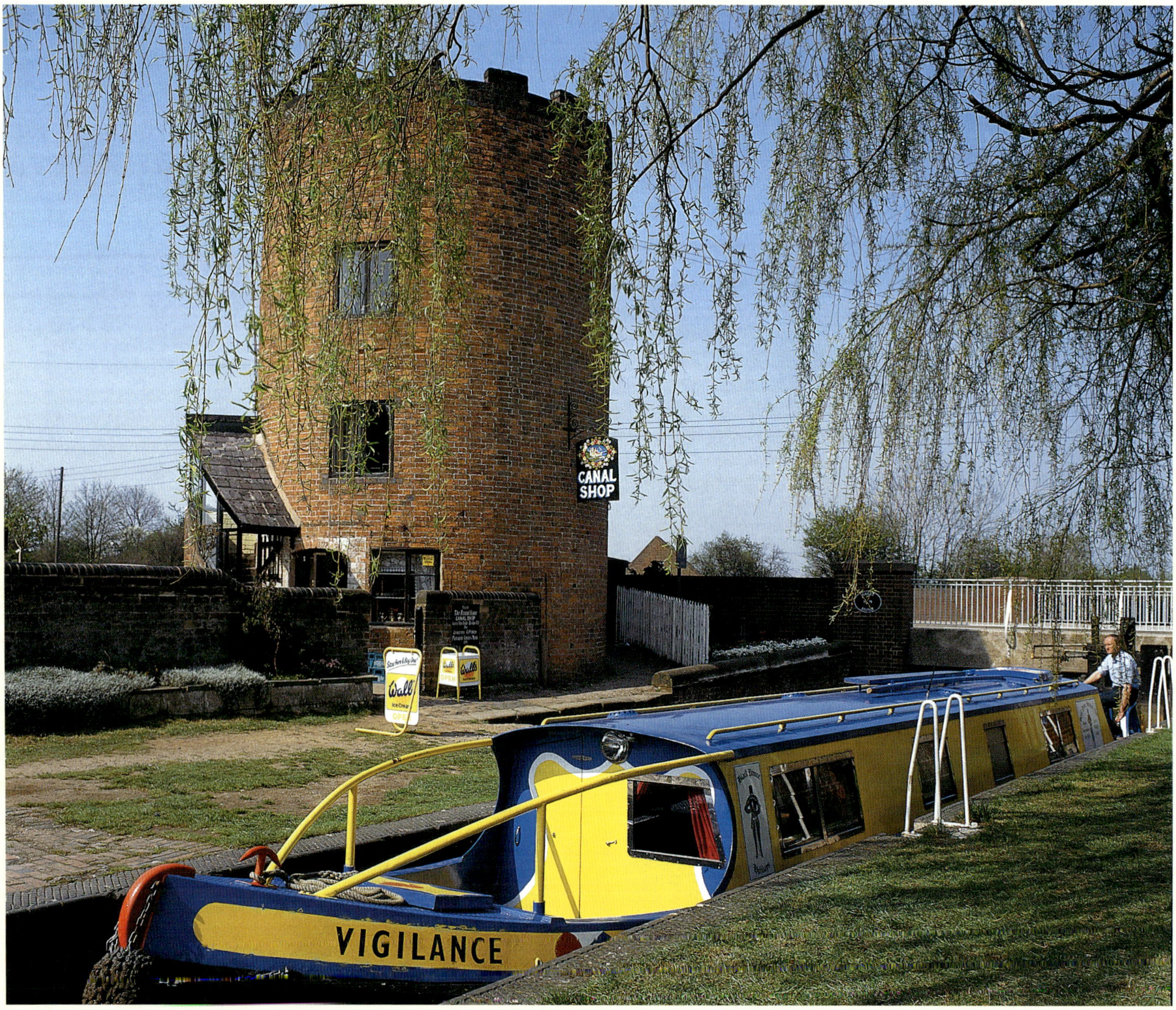
CANAL SHOP
VIGILANCE

Invention & Ingenuity

The canal system never lacks in a capacity to surprise and delight. Ingenuity was the by-word of 18th century engineering and individual functionalism often resulted in structures of great beauty and curiousity. The Mariners Chapel, **Gloucester Docks** *(opposite upper)* is still occasionally used for services, though one suspects that matelots no longer figure prominently in the congregation.

The Round House at **Gailey** *(opposite lower)* on the Staffordshire & Worcestershire Canal, is now home to an excellent canal shop, but originally was used as accommodation by the toll-clerk, supposedly to offer him a clear view of the canal in either direction. The Staffordshire & Worcestershire Canal also features characteristic circular weirs such as this one *(below left)* by **Stewponey Lock**.

An air shaft *(right)* towers over the open countryside above **Blisworth Tunnel** in Northamptonshire.

Springtime at **Chalford** *(below right)* on the Thames & Severn Canal and daffodils provide a colourful foreground to one of the circular lock-keeper's houses that are a picturesque feature of this yet to be restored canal.

At **Kings Norton**, south-west of Birmingham, you come upon this strangely curious guillotine-like structure *(right)* which was formerly a lock built to separate the precious water supplies of two distinct canal companies, the Worcester & Birmingham Canal and the Stratford-on-Avon Canal. Though it is no longer in operational use, it is worth seeking out for the sheer incongruity of its engineering.

From the ridiculous to the sublime! The famous **Boat Lift at Anderton** *(below)* is generally recognised as the UK canal network's most important piece of machinery. It was opened in 1875 to facilitate the passage of boats between the Trent & Mersey Canal and the Weaver Navigation. At Anderton on the outskirts of Northwich the two waterways are only yards apart but separated by a gulf of 50 feet. Locks were not a practical option, and so Sir Edward Leader-Williams designed a steam operated lifting mechanism consisting of two giant water tanks into which boats could be floated prior to being raised or lowered between the two routes. It operated successfully for over a hundred years - having been converted to electrical power in 1903 - but corrosion rendered it unfit for working in 1983. Almost twenty years elapsed before it was rightfully restored to use. Now it is one of the region's premier tourist attractions boasting a visitor centre and trip boat operations.

Another of Leader-Williams's designs is **Barton Swing Aqueduct** *(opposite upper)* which carries the Bridgewater Canal across the Manchester Ship Canal at Barton upon Irwell near Eccles on the outskirts of Manchester. It dates from 1894 and had a requirement to swing so as to enable ocean-going shipping to reach the docks at Salford and Manchester, a mile or two upstream. Sadly, a decline in shipping movements on the Ship Canal means that it doesn't need to swing quite so often as in the busier past, but by any standards it is a remarkable piece of engineering, just a tram ride and a brisk walk out from central Manchester.

If you were thinking that all canal engineering dates from the 18th and 19th centuries, then it's time you got yourself up to central Scotland to visit the remarkable Falkirk Wheel, a 21st century response to a similar problem faced by Leader-Williams at Anderton. The **Falkirk Wheel** *(below)* connects the recently fully restored Forth & Clyde and Union canals. As at Anderton, there are boat trips to be enjoyed together with a visitor centre to explore, and you are left to marvel that a new canal age is perhaps just about to dawn.

Tucked away in the backstreets of **Huddersfield** (*above*) is one of the most peculiar contraptions on the whole of the inland waterways, Locomotive Bridge. It functions as a lift bridge, hand-winched to the raised position by boaters before their vessels can pass. As the final item in this book it merely serves to emphasise the wonder of the waterways and their inherent ability to conjour up the most surprising features in the least expected places. The moral is go and explore the system for yourself, you never know what's round the next canal corner, and you'll enjoy every minute of it. Have fun!